THESEUS
BATTLING THE MINOTAUR

A GREEK MYTH

STORY BY
JEFF LIMKE

PENCILS AND INKS BY
JOHN McCREA

EUROPE

ITALY

MEDITERRANEAN SEA

THESEUS

BATTLING THE MINOTAUR

A
GREEK
MYTH

BLACK SEA

GREECE

AEGEAN SEA

ATHENS

TURKEY

CRETE

GRAPHIC UNIVERSE™•MINNEAPOLIS

THESEUS IS ONE OF THE GREATEST HEROES OF GREEK MYTHOLOGY. HIS FEATS OF STRENGTH AND COURAGE HAVE BEEN PASSED DOWN FROM GENERATION TO GENERATION FOR MORE THAN 2000 YEARS. THIS PARTICULAR BOOK FOLLOWS THESEUS' EARLY ADVENTURES, AS HE COMES OF AGE AND ATTEMPTS TO FULFILL HIS DESTINY AS A GREAT HERO AND ATHENS' GREATEST KING. TO CRAFT THIS TALE FOR THE GRAPHIC MYTHS AND LEGENDS SERIES, AUTHOR JEFF LIMKE CONSULTED TWO OF THE MOST FAMOUS ANTHOLOGIES OF GREEK MYTHS, EDITH HAMILTON'S *MYTHOLOGY* AND *BULFINCH'S MYTHOLOGY* BY THOMAS BULFINCH. ARTIST JOHN McCREA REFERENCED NUMEROUS HISTORICAL AND TRADITIONAL SOURCES TO GIVE THE ART AN AUTHENTIC LOOK, FROM CLASSICAL GREEK ARCHITECTURE TO THE CLOTHING, WEAPONS, AND ARMOR WORN BY THE CHARACTERS. PROFESSOR DAVID MULROY ENSURED HISTORICAL AND VISUAL ACCURACY.

STORY BY JEFF LIMKE

PENCILS AND INKS BY JOHN McCREA

COLORING BY HI-FI COLOUR DESIGN

LETTERING BY HI-FI COLOUR DESIGN

CONSULTANT: DAVID MULROY, PH.D.
UNIVERSITY OF WISCONSIN-MILWAUKEE

Graphic Universe™
A division of Lerner Publishing Group, Inc.
241 First Avenue North
Minneapolis, MN 55401 U.S.A.

Website address: www.lernerbooks.com

Library of Congress Cataloging-in-Publication Data

Limke, Jeff.
    Theseus : battling the Minotaur / by Jeff Limke ; illustrations by John McCrea.
        p.   cm. — (Graphic myths and legends)
    Includes index.
        ISBN 978-0-8225-6756-1 (lib. bdg. : alk. paper)
        1. Theseus (Greek mythology)—Juvenile literature.
    2. Minotaur (Greek mythology)—Juvenile literature.
    I. McCrea, John, artist/creator. II. Title.
    BL820.T5L56 2008
    741.5'973—dc22
                                                                    2007001829

TABLE OF CONTENTS

THE TREASURE BENEATH THE BOULDER

MY NAME IS *CONNIDUS* AND I TAUGHT *THESEUS* AS A CHILD. I TAUGHT HIM HISTORY, POETRY, AND MATHEMATICS. HIS MOTHER *AETHRA* TAUGHT HIM WHAT HE NEEDED TO KNOW TO BECOME KING. WHAT HE NEEDED TO LEARN TO BECOME ONE OF GREECE'S GREATEST HEROES, HE WOULD HAVE TO LEARN ON HIS OWN.

WHEN HE WAS OLD ENOUGH, HIS MOTHER TOLD HIM THAT THE FIRST OF MANY TASKS HE WOULD HAVE TO PERFORM WOULD BE TO MOVE THE BOULDER THAT STOOD AT THE TOP OF THE HILL ABOVE THE CAVE WHERE HE LIVED.

WHAT SHE DIDN'T TELL HIM WAS THAT HIS FATHER WAS THE CURRENT KING OF ATHENS. INSTEAD SHE HAD TOLD HIM HE WAS THE SON OF *POSEIDON*, THE GOD OF THE SEA.

THE TREASURE BENEATH THE ROCK WAS *NOT* WHAT HE HAD EXPECTED.

THE KING OF ATHENS

SEND A MESSENGER TO THE PALACE! A LONE MAN CARRYING A WEAPON APPROACHES.

WHAT NEWS DO YOU BRING ME?

A LONE TRAVELER ARRIVES!

THAT IS NOT NEWS!

MAKE WAY, I HAVE AN URGENT MESSAGE FOR THE KING!

BUT THIS TRAVELER CARRIES A WEAPON OF ONE OF THE BANDITS KNOWN TO LIVE ON THE ROAD TO ATHENS.

THIS I MUST SEE.

TAKE ME TO SEE HIM.

TELL ME YOUR NAME, BOY.

MY MOTHER NAMED ME *THESEUS*.

AND THIS CLUB? IT BELONGED TO *CORYNETES* DIDN'T IT?

YES. IT'S MINE NOW.

I DON'T THINK HE'LL BE BOTHERING ANY MORE TRAVELERS.

SO I HEAR. MY SOLDIERS TELL ME YOU HAVE MADE TRAVEL SAFE ON THAT ROAD.

YOU HAVE MY THANKS.

YOU'RE A GUEST IN MY PALACE.

THAT SIGN ON THE SHIELD IS THE SAME AS *AEGEUS'*.

THESEUS IS KING *AEGEUS'* SON.

LATER, *AEGEUS* INVITED THE NOBLES TO A GREAT BANQUET TO TALK, TO EAT, AND TO INTRODUCE THEM TO THE YOUNG HERO WHO HAD MADE THE ROAD SAFE.

YOUNG *THESEUS.* WHO ARE YOUR PARENTS, AGAIN?

I DIDN'T KNOW MY FATHER. I WAS TOLD IT WAS *POSEIDON*, BUT HE HAS NEVER VISITED ME.

BUT MY MOTHER'S NAME WAS—

—AETHRA

SAY THAT NAME AGAIN, BOY!

AETHRA?

DON'T LET HIM DRINK THAT—

—AND BRING HIM TO ME!

TELL ME MORE.

THE BOY SHOULD KNOW, AEGEUS.

VERY WELL.

EVERY YEAR WE SEND SEVEN BOYS AND SEVEN GIRLS SO CRETE WILL NOT WAGE WAR AGAINST US.

I DO NOT LIKE DOING THIS, BUT WE WOULD LOSE MORE LIVES IF KING MINOS ATTACKED US AS HE DID BEFORE THIS AGREEMENT.

WE HEAR TALES OF WHAT HAPPENS TO THEM, BUT NO ONE HAS EVER RETURNED ALIVE TO TELL US FOR SURE.

MY SONS ARE TOO YOUNG, BUT YOU—

—YOU COULD BE THE HERO TO END THIS TERRIBLE THING.

INCLUDE ME WITH THIS OFFERING.

I CAN END THIS!

PUT ME ON THE SHIP. I AM NOT TOO OLD TO DO THIS.

LET THE PEOPLE KNOW I AM GOING.

THEY WILL KNOW YOU ARE ONE OF THEM BY SACRIFICING YOUR ONLY SON.

BUT YOU HAVE JUST RETURNED. I CAN'T SEND YOU AWAY NOW.

YOU MUST. I CAN UNITE THE PEOPLE FOR YOU—

—FOR US.

25

BE SAFE.

I WILL BE, FATHER. ONE WAY OR ANOTHER I WILL END THIS.

YOU SPEAK LIKE A RULER.

LET'S HOPE THAT I HAVE THE CHANCE TO BE ONE.

LET'S HOPE NOT.

I ONLY HAVE ONE REQUEST. IF EVERYTHING HAS GONE WELL AND YOU RETURN, HAVE THE CAPTAIN FLY A WHITE SAIL.

IF YOU DON'T RETURN, MAKE SURE THE CAPTAIN FLIES A BLACK SAIL.

I WILL.

AND SO THE SHIP SAILED FOR THE ISLAND OF CRETE'S CAPITAL, *KNOSSOS*, RULED BY *KING MINOS*.

TAKE HIM AWAY.

HE WILL BE THE FIRST IN THE LABYRINTH TOMORROW. WE'LL SEE IF HE CAN BE THE FIRST TO OUTWIT ITS DESIGNER, *DAEDALUS.*

YOU BETTER BE READY FOR TOMORROW.

YEAH, YOU'RE GOING TO MEET THE MINOTAUR.

OOOH, YOU'RE GOING TO BE HIS BREAKFAST!

WHAT'S A MINOTAUR?

I DON'T KNOW.

AREN'T YOU SCARED?

NO. I'M NOT SCARED OF SOMETHING I DON'T KNOW.

YOU SHOULD BE.

WHO ARE YOU? DO YOU KNOW WHAT THE MINOTAUR IS?

MY NAME IS *ARIADNE.* MY FATHER *KING MINOS* HAD DAEDALUS DESIGN THE LABYRINTH TO KEEP THE MINOTAUR IMPRISONED AND AWAY FROM US.

THE MINOTAUR IS A THING CHILDREN OF CRETE HAVE NIGHTMARES ABOUT.

IF ONLY *THESEUS* HAD KNOWN THE GODDESS *APHRODITE* HAD SMILED ON HIM. THE GODDESS OF LOVE HAD MADE SURE HE WOULD HAVE HELP WHEN HE NEEDED IT.

IT'S A SAD TALE.

MY STEPMOTHER *PASIPHAË* WAS WITH CHILD.

THE LABOR HAD BEEN LONG AND PAINFUL. HER SERVANT WOMEN WEREN'T SURE SHE WOULD SURVIVE.

BUT SHE DID AND SO DID HER CHILD. BUT NO ONE EXPECTED HIM TO LOOK LIKE–

–THIS!

MINOS REFUSED TO ADMIT THE CHILD WAS HIS.

IN FACT, HE WAS SO *EMBARRASSED* HE WOULD HAVE *NOTHING* TO DO WITH IT.

MINOS WENT TO THE TEMPLE TO FIND OUT WHAT TO DO WITH THE MONSTER.

HE RECEIVED MANY DIFFERENT SUGGESTIONS.

MOST SAID HE SHOULD DESTROY THE MONSTER. BUT HE COULDN'T DO THAT. HE KNEW THE GODS WOULD CURSE HIM IF HE KILLED HIS OWN CHILD.

29

ONE PRIEST TOLD HIM TO BUILD A MAZE IN THE EARTH FROM WHICH THE MONSTER COULD NEVER ESCAPE.

MINOS THOUGHT THE PRIEST WAS A FOOL. BUT THE PRIEST WARNED HIM THE MONSTER WOULD EAT PEOPLE AND RUN WILD IF NOT KEPT CAPTIVE.

SO, MY FATHER CAPTURED DAEDALUS. MINOS FORCED HIM TO BUILD A LABYRINTH, OR MAZE, THAT THE MINOTAUR COULD NOT ESCAPE.

DAEDALUS IS THE SMARTEST MAN IN THE WORLD. HE HAD MANY OTHER THINGS HE WOULD RATHER HAVE DONE.

BUT HE WAS MINOS' PRISONER, SO HE HAD NO CHOICE.

I BEFRIENDED DAEDALUS. HE TOOK CARE OF ME WHILE THE LABYRINTH WAS BEING BUILT.

I GOT TO KNOW MY HALF-BROTHER. HE WAS NOT AS SMART AS THE OTHER CHILDREN AND HE HAD A TERRIBLE TEMPER.

HE WAS NICE TO ME, BUT HE WAS NEVER LET OUT OF HIS CAGE.

THE FINISHED LABYRINTH WAS EVERYTHING MINOS HAD WANTED.

DAEDALUS GUARANTEED THAT NO ONE WOULD EVER BE ABLE TO FIND THE WAY OUT UNAIDED.

THEY PUT THE MINOTAUR INSIDE.

I FELT VERY SORRY FOR HIM. HE DIDN'T DESERVE TO BE KEPT LIKE THAT.

NO ONE SHOULD HAVE TO LIVE LIKE THAT.

30

33

MROOOAA!

RRAWRR!

THESEUS' LUNGS BURNED, HIS RIBS ACHED AND IT HURT TO STAND.

HE HAD GIVEN THE MONSTER HIS BEST SO FAR, YET THE BEAST WOULD NOT STAY DOWN.

TWACK!!

UNH...

41

RETURN TO ATHENS

*T*HE BOYS AND GIRLS WHO HAD COME WITH ***THESEUS*** CELEBRATED TOGETHER ON THE SHIP.

THEY WERE BEYOND HAPPY KNOWING THEY WOULD RETURN HOME TO THEIR FAMILIES.

THEY CELEBRATED THE WHOLE WAY WITHOUT A WORRY IN THEIR HEARTS.

HAVE THERE BEEN *ANY* SIGHTINGS?

A SHIP IS ON THE HORIZON, BUT NO ONE IS SURE.

BUT WHAT OF THE SAIL?

WE JUST CAN'T TELL.

WHAT COLOR IS THE SAIL?

MY KING, MY KING. WE CAN SEE THE SHIP!

IT IS *BLACK!*

YOU MUST BE WRONG!

I MUST SEE IT MYSELF.

MY KING! BE CAREFUL SO YOU DON'T–

NOOOOOO!

BE CAREFUL, *FOOLS*, THOSE BOYS ARE THE NEW RULERS!

YES, *QUEEN MEDEA.*

NOW TO GREET THOSE WHO HAVE—

THESEUS!

THESEUS!

THESEUS!

THESEUS!

STEPMOTHER, WHERE IS MY FATHER?

B-BUT YOUR *SAILS...*

WE *THOUGHT...*

...MY CHILDREN WERE *SUPPOSED* TO BE...

...THE SAIL WAS BLACK!

THESEUS, YOUR FATHER HAS *DIED.*

WHAT?!

YOU ARE THE KING OF ATHENS NOW.

MEDEA HAD DISAPPEARED WITH HER SONS BEFORE THE FUNERAL OF *AEGEUS.*

THESEUS BROUGHT HIS TRUE FAMILY TO LIVE WITH HIM IN ATHENS.

THEY BURIED *AEGEUS* WITHIN THE ROYAL FAMILY'S TOMB.

44

THESEUS HAD PROVED TO HIMSELF THAT HE COULD BE A HERO.

NOW HE WOULD HAVE TO PROVE TO HIS PEOPLE THAT HE COULD BE A HEROIC KING.

GLOSSARY AND PRONUNCIATION GUIDE

AEGEUS (eh-*jee*-us): the king of Athens and Theseus' father

AETHRA (*ee*-thrah): Aegeus' wife and Theseus' mother

APHRODITE (a-fruh-*dy*-tee): the Greek goddess of love and beauty

ARIADNE (ah-ree-*ad*-nee): Minos' daughter, who helps Theseus to escape the labyrinth

ATHENS (*a*-thenz): one of the great historic Greek city states

CONNIDUS (kun-*eye*-duhs): Theseus' centaur (half-horse, half-human) tutor

CRETE (kreet): a large island in the eastern Mediterranean Sea, off the southern coast of Greece

DAEDALUS (*deh*-deh-lus): the engineering genius who built the labyrinth for King Minos

HERAKLES (*hair*-uh-kleez): a legendary Greek hero; also known by his Roman name, Hercules

LABYRINTH (*la*-buh-rinth): a place full of confusing passageways and dead ends; a maze

MEDEA (muh-*dee*-uh): Aegeus' wife

MINOS (*my*-nohs): the king of Crete and the father of the Minotaur and of Ariadne

MINOTAUR (*my*-nuh-tor): a ferocious half-man, half-bull; the son of Minos and Pasiphaë

PASIPHAË (pas-uh-*fay*): wife of Minos, mother of the Minotaur

PERIPHETES (puh-reh-*fee*-teez): a bandit who preys on travelers along the road to Athens

PITTHEUS (pit-*thee*-us): Theseus' grandfather

POSEIDON (poh-*sy*-duhn): the Greek god of the sea

PROCRUSTES (proh-*krus*-teez): an evil innkeeper who murders his guests by stretching them or cutting off their limbs

SINIS (*sin*-uhs): a sinister bandit who kills his victims by forcing them to hold the tops of two trees at the same time, causing them to be torn apart

THESEUS (*thee*-see-uhs): son of Aegeus and Aethra; Aegeus' successor as king of Athens

FURTHER READING, WEBSITES, AND MOVIES

Bolton, Lesley. *The Everything Classical Mythology Book: Greek and Roman Gods, Goddesses, Heroes, and Monsters from Ares to Zeus.* Avon, MA: Adams Media Corporation, 2002. This who's who guide introduces young readers to Greek and Roman mythology.

Day, Nancy. *Your Travel Guide to Ancient Greece.* Minneapolis: Twenty-First Century Books, 2001. Day prepares readers for a trip back to ancient Greece, including which cities to visit, how to get around, what to wear, and how to fit in with the locals.

Jim Henson's The Storyteller: Greek Myths. DVD. Directed by David Garfath and John Madden. Hollywood, CA: Sony Pictures, 2004. In this entertaining series of stories, four famous Greek myths—including Theseus and the Minotaur—are brought to life using live actors and puppets.

Limke, Jeff. *Jason: Quest for the Golden Fleece.* Minneapolis: Graphic Universe, 2007. Read about the exciting adventures of another great Greek hero, Jason, and his relationship with a certain woman named Medea.

MythWeb. http://www.mythweb.com/index.html. This site, with a searchable encyclopedia, provides students with information on gods, goddesses, and places in Greek myth, as well as ample information about Theseus.

Storrie, Paul D. *Hercules: The Twelve Labors.* Minneapolis: Graphic Universe, 2007. Learn about Theseus' hero and inspiration, Hercules, one of Greece's greatest legends.

CREATING *THESEUS: BATTLING THE MINOTAUR*

To craft this tale for the Graphic Myths and Legends series, author Jeff Limke consulted two of the most famous anthologies of Greek myths, Edith Hamilton's *Mythology* and *Bulfinch's Mythology* by Thomas Bulfinch. Artist John McCrea referenced numerous historical and traditional sources to give the art and authentic look, from classical Greek architecture to the clothing, weapons, and armor worn by the characters. Professor David Mulroy ensured historical and visual accuracy.

original pencil from page 15

INDEX

ABOUT THE AUTHOR AND THE ARTIST

JEFF LIMKE was raised in North Dakota. There he read, listened to, and marveled at stories from the day he learned to read. He later taught stories for many years and has written adaptations of them. Some of his stories have been published by Arrow Comics, Caliber Comics, and Kenzer and Company. His titles for Graphic Universe include *King Arthur: Excalibur Unsheathed*; *Isis & Osiris: To the Ends of the Earth*; *Thor & Loki: In the Land of Giants*; *Jason: The Quest for the Golden Fleece*; and *Arthur & Lancelot: The Fight for Camelot*. Along the way, he got married, and he and his wife had a daughter who loves to read, listen to, and marvel at stories.

JOHN McCREA was born in Belfast, Northern Ireland. He has been drawing comics professionally for nearly twenty years. His work has become well known through comics for both DC and Marvel, including titles for such series as *Judge Dredd*, *Hitman*, and *Section 8*. He currently lives in Birmingham, England.